TIM ROSS

UPSET THE WORLD

STUDY GUIDE

GATEWAY® PRESS

Upset the World Study Guide

ISBN Paperback: 978-1-951227-08-1
ISBN eBook: 978-1-951227-19-7

We hope you hear from the Holy Spirit and receive God's richest blessings from this book by Gateway Press. We want to provide the highest quality resources that take the messages, music, and media of Gateway Church to the world. For more information on other resources from Gateway Publishing®, go to gatewaypublishing.com.

Gateway Press, an imprint of Gateway Publishing
700 Blessed Way
Southlake, TX 76092
gatewaypublishing.com

Printed in the United States of America

20 21 22 23 — 5 4 3 2 1

TABLE OF CONTENTS

INTRODUCTION

Lord, help me be an upsetter. Amen.

M ost people don't like to be upset, especially if that means they are going to be angry. There is more than enough anger in the world already. However, God has used His chosen people to upset the world from the very beginning. Faithful servants and prophets like Noah, Moses, David, Joshua, and many others upset the ancient world as they prepared the way for God's ultimate upset: the coming in power of Jesus Christ, the Messiah and Savior of the world. The purpose of *Upset the World* is to help you be like Jesus.

No figure in the Bible upset things more than Jesus. However, while Jesus' teaching certainly evoked anger in some of those He encountered, that is not the primary meaning of *upset* in the biblical context, and that is not what He called His disciples to do.

In Acts 16 Paul and Silas are imprisoned in Philippi for their evangelizing, but they are released after their prayers cause a massive earthquake that shakes open the prison doors and causes their chains to fall off. In

Acts 17 Paul and Silas are in Thessalonica, again causing all kinds of disturbances among the Jews by teaching Christ publicly in the synagogue. Their teaching causes many Jews, along with some Greek men and women, to believe Jesus is the Messiah and become followers of Christ.

An angry mob eventually looks for Paul and Silas in Jason's house, and not finding them there, they drag Jason and some other believers in front of the city council. Verse 6 describes how the people felt: "Paul and Silas have caused trouble all over the world," they shouted, "and now they are here disturbing our city, too." Verse 8 says, "The people of the city, as well as the city council, were thrown into turmoil by these reports."

In the Greek, the word *trouble* literally means 'upset,' so this verse should read, "Paul and Silas upset the world." Rather than causing anger, the more accurate and appropriate definition of upset is 'to disturb or derange completely.'

When you come into a relationship with Jesus Christ, your world is disturbed and deranged completely. He has come into your life and turned the whole thing upside down or, more accurately, right side up. An upsetter is a person who has been upset by the overwhelming love of Jesus and upsets others. The person who came to upset us is also the One who shows us how to *upset the world*.

This study guide will lead you through each chapter of the book, expanding on the material and challenging your thinking with examples and questions. At the end of each chapter you will find Activation exercises to help put principles into practice.

Paul and Silas upset—completely disturbed and deranged—people with the message, hope, and love of Jesus Christ. And *this* is the assignment Jesus gives to each and every one of us, His believers: that we, as His sons and daughters, would upset the world with the message, hope, and love of Jesus Christ.

It's my prayer that this book will ignite you to live your life as an upsetter—a person who will go out and share the love of Christ in the most relational way possible— so you too can *upset the world*.

God will reward your efforts as you allow the Holy Spirit to help you fulfill Jesus' Great Commission to "go and make disciples of all the nations" (Matthew 28:19).

CHAPTER 1
UPSETTERS MUST BE UPSET FIRST

God, upset me. Amen.

Key Scriptures: John 3:16; Ephesians 4:1–5

As a pastor's child growing up just outside of Los Angeles, I was at church all the time. If the doors were open, I was there.

After graduating from high school, I would still go to church, but more out of habit rather than relationship. My true passion was spending time with my friends and performing almost every weekend as a rapper around different parts of the city.

Have you ever spent time doing things out of habit or a feeling of obligation because of the expectations of others, such as parents, friends, or other authority figures? What were the circumstances? Why do you think you acted that way?

_____

_____

_____

_____

_____

When you did these habitual things, did it ever bother you? Explain.

_____

_____

_____

_____

_____

On January 14, 1996, God changed my life forever. That Sunday night I sat in the back of the church, and without hearing a sermon or invitation, the Holy Spirit convicted me of my sins and the need to change my life. I gave my life to Jesus. My life was totally *upset.*

When my friends came to pick me up after service, as they usually did, I told my brother Myles, who had skipped church that day, about my experience. He and my friends left me behind and went to the beach without me.

Myles and my friends were actually respecting my decision. They knew something was different about me now, and it was upsetting them. Since they weren't ready to deal with it and change, they left me alone.

Have you ever had someone close to you change their behavior toward you because of a personal decision you made? What were the circumstances?

_____

_____

_____

_____

Everything changed when I fell in love with God. He transformed my heart. In doing so, I had become upset in the best possible way.

What does it mean to no longer rely on your own will when you fall in love with God?

_____

_____

_____

_____

WHY BE UPSET

After you enter a relationship with Jesus, the way you live will change. Living your life the way God wants you to live it will probably throw your life into chaos and disorder—*it will upset your world*!

What habits changed when you came into a relationship with Jesus? Did you make new choices and start associating with different people? Explain.

_____

_____

_____

_____

Think of some other people you know who experienced this saving power. What changes did you see in them?

_____

_____

_____

_____

According to Ephesians 1:4, when did God begin to love us?

_____

_____

_____

_____

According to verse 5, what did God plan to do for us and why did He want to do it? What does that tell us about Jesus' purpose in coming to earth? Why should that *upset* us?

_____

_____

_____

_____

JESUS CAME TO UPSET THE WORLD

Jesus so upset the whole world that we are still talking about Him 2,019 years later.

What are some evidences for how Jesus has upset the entire world?

_____

_____

_____

_____

Whose plans did Jesus come to the earth to upset? What five things did He come to bring us?

_____

_____

_____

_____

When you are strongly affected by an emotion, it's hard not to let other people know about it. What experience or emotion from your past have you felt like you had to make known? What did you do about it?

_____

_____

_____

_____

When you are truly upset by Jesus, and people are around you for a while, they won't be able to avoid having their worlds upset as well.

Explain this sentence: "The person who came to upset us is also the One who shows us how to upset the world."

_____

_____

_____

_____

JESUS UPSETS SAUL

If there was ever a New Testament example of someone who needed to be upset, it was Saul.

Saul was going everywhere to destroy the church. He went from house to house, dragging out both men and women to throw them into prison (Acts 8:3).

Paul was so enraged against Christians that he was willing to travel 225 miles from Jerusalem to Damascus just so he could bring them back to Jerusalem and lock them up. Of course, while on his way there, something happened that completely changed his life.

Read Acts 9:3–9. What spirit was Jesus trying to upset in Paul's life through this miraculous event?

_____

_____

_____

_____

Saul was blinded, and the men with him were struck speechless because they could hear the voice but see nobody. Saul only said four words (Who are you, lord? (v. 5)) during this entire encounter with Jesus. Then he was led to Damascus by the hand and did not eat or drink for three days.

What do you think Paul thought and felt during that final entry into Damascus and the three days of waiting? How do you think you would have reacted?

_____

_____

_____

_____

When Ananias laid his hands on Saul, he was filled with the Holy Spirit and his sight was restored.

What did Saul do upon receiving the Holy Spirit? How long did he wait before he began testifying and preaching about Jesus?

Read Acts 9:20. Where did Saul preach about Jesus—whom would he have been preaching to? Why is the location of his preaching significant?

_____

_____

_____

_____

_____

How do you think those who heard Saul in the synagogues—especially the religious leaders—reacted when they first heard Saul preach that Jesus is indeed the Son of God?

_____

_____

_____

_____

_____

Note that verse 22 says that the Jews "could not refute his proofs that Jesus was indeed the Messiah." What do you think this meant in practice? What "proofs" would Saul have been able to provide considering that he had been a murderer of Christians just days before?

_____

_____

_____

_____

_____

Saul is no different than many people in our time who are atheists, agnostics, or radicalized in their own religion. God still has the power to upset the lives of those who are caught up in a religious spirit and bring them to the Messiah.

C. S. Lewis is an example of a proclaimed atheist and scholar who was not only brought to faith in Jesus but also became a powerful disciple. What other modern-day examples can you find who were converted from atheism or another religion, or were strongly anti-Christian, and became powerful "preachers in the synagogues"?

_____

_____

_____

_____

_____

JESUS UPSETS PETER

In Luke chapter 5, we read the story of Peter and Jesus at the Sea of Galilee. Whereas Jesus upsetting Paul dealt with the spirit of religion, what spirit did Jesus come to disrupt and upset in this story in Luke?

_____

_____

_____

_____

_____

What was Peter's response when Jesus asked Peter to use one of his boats to go out on the sea and preach?

_____

_____

_____

_____

_____

What was Peter's response when, after Jesus finished preaching, He suggested to Peter that they go out fishing? Why, in a practical sense, did Peter respond this way?

_____

_____

_____

_____

_____

What was the real, underlying reason that Peter reacted the way he did? How did Peter's history and experience contribute to this reaction?

_____

_____

_____

_____

_____

When you give your life to Jesus, everything changes, and everything in your life belongs to Him. Your life is turned upside down from what the world says is normal. So when the Holy Spirit nudges you, you need to listen.

Describe a time in your life where the Holy Spirit (whether it be directly or through your conscience) nudged you to do something. How did you respond? If you resisted, what was the result?

_____

_____

_____

_____

_____

Against their better judgment, Peter and his friends went out into the lake in the middle of the night and threw their nets into the deep water. What miraculous event happened next? What was Peter's response to seeing this miracle (see Luke 5:8)?

_____

_____

_____

_____

_____

Read Luke 5:9–11. What was the response of the other fishermen in the boat? What was the reason (the characteristic of Jesus) that drew these men, especially Peter, to Jesus?

_____

_____

_____

_____

_____

Do you tend to be a confident person who knows the right way to do things? What is the only way that Jesus can break off our spirit of independence?

_____

_____

_____

_____

_____

YOU MUST BE UPSET FIRST

After Saul and Peter were upset by Jesus—Saul's religious spirit and Peter's spirit of independence—what did they both immediately begin to tell others?

_____

_____

_____

_____

_____

What are some of the reasons people may feel apprehensive about sharing their testimonies? Are those reasons valid? Explain.

_____

_____

_____

_____

_____

What is the only thing that you need to begin sharing your story and declaring that Jesus Christ is Lord? What are some of the reasons people might think they need to wait before they share their story?

_____

_____

_____

_____

What was the reaction of the girl I was dating when I told her the good news of giving my life to Christ? Describe my response to her.

_____

_____

_____

_____

What are some of the changes that occur when your life has been truly upset by the overwhelming love of God?

_____

_____

_____

_____

UPSETTERS LOVE JESUS

The reason you can't upset the world until you've been upset is that upsetters love Jesus.

What kind of love or expressions of love are truly indic-ative of the changed heart of an upsetter? Explain.

_____

_____

_____

_____

Obviously, we all have different personalities, emotions, and experiences. How did you personally respond to your conversion and faith in Christ? Were you more outgoing or reserved? Explain.

_____

_____

_____

_____

You can't be an upsetter without loving Jesus because only people who love are infectious. People only follow people who are really passionate about something or someone. Describe some examples where you have seen this demonstrated.

_____

_____

_____

_____

When we fall in love with Jesus, our passionate response will evoke a response in others that might shock people who would never expect to see that passion in you. And that response will help make you an example to upset others.

Activation

- Ask your friends or family members what changes they noticed in your life when you became a Christian.
- Is there any area of your life where you are struggling to give control over to Jesus? If yes, ask God to help you surrender that area today.

CHAPTER 2
UPSETTERS LOVE PEOPLE

Holy Spirit, help me love people so I can upset them. Amen,

Key Scriptures: Matthew 5:43–48; Proverbs 25:21–22

Years ago, my friend Janette got me a job as a temp at a leading advertising agency in Los Angeles. That is where I met Mary (not her real name). Mary was no more than five feet tall, but despite her small stature, she had an oversized reputation as a feared supervisor. Everyone was afraid of Mary.

What was the unique way that our coworkers always knew when Mary had arrived at the office?

_____

_____

_____

_____

My first impression of Mary was that she was a sweet little lady. Janette quickly filled me in, however, as to Mary's many unpleasant characteristics. Rather than engaging in conflict, I asked Janette and some other believers at the office to engage in spiritual warfare on Mary's behalf.

Have you ever had a coworker or acquaintance who you thought was just too unpleasant to be around or develop any kind of relationship with? What were the circumstances?

_____

_____

_____

_____

What were the actions we took to "go after" Mary in spiritual warfare?

_____

_____

_____

_____

_____

What was the result after the first week of praying for Mary?

_____

_____

_____

_____

_____

What gradually happened during the second week of continuing prayer for Mary? How do you explain her change in temperament and even offering to buy lunch that Friday?

_____

_____

_____

_____

_____

After the third week of prayer, Mary started asking us to pray for her. She and Janette became close friends and started attending Bible classes together.

What effect do you think this series of events had on Janette? On the other employees in the office?

_____

_____

_____

_____

Simply put, how had we completely upset Mary's world?

_____

_____

_____

_____

Do you tend to stay away from people that are mean or unpleasant or make you feel uncomfortable? How about people who are different from you?

_____

_____

_____

_____

Have you ever "gone after" someone in prayer? What were the results?

_____

_____

_____

_____

If we are constantly huddled in the corner with our safe, Christian friends, how will others get a chance to see us or experience the blessings that we as Christians already know about? Is there someone that you have held back from knowing that you might be able to become a blessing to?

_____

_____

_____

_____

Quite honestly, we spend a lot of time talking to each other before we talk to God. I think if we talked to God first, we would have less to say to each other about how different we are and more to say about how we're alike.

LOVE EVERYBODY

We live in one of the most racially charged, politically crazy times in our country's history. We can easily get angry and worked up by people who have different opinions, and then share them instantly—and sometimes thoughtlessly—on social media.

Read Matthew 5:43–48. Summarize in your own words Jesus' commands for us in this passage.

_____

_____

_____

_____

Upsetters must love all kinds of people with different political views. They love people who hate them and despise them. They love people who are unlovable.

As upsetters, the only way that we can truly love people who don't love us is to love Jesus first.

Think of someone you know who is particularly unlovable. How difficult is it for you to show love to that person? How do you deal with that feeling and the person?

_____

_____

_____

_____

_____

You change the power of the atmosphere around you by taking on the attitude of Jesus: "I'm just going to love people the way You did!" You don't have to like or approve of them; just love them right where they are. You respond to them with the nature and will of Jesus rather than your own.

Why, when Jesus went around doing good for people, was it so difficult for the religious leaders to accept Him and His good deeds?

_____

_____

_____

_____

_____

Read Luke 10:25–37. What is the significance that the man who confronted Jesus was a religious expert? How did he try to manipulate Jesus with his question about what he needed to do to inherit eternal life (v. 25)?

_____

_____

_____

_____

How did Jesus put the ball back in the religious expert's court?

_____

_____

_____

_____

Which Scripture passages from Deuteronomy and Leviticus did he use to respond to Jesus?

_____

_____

_____

_____

What Jesus did was let the Scripture speak for Him. The point was simply that if you really love God, then you _can_ love your neighbor. To put it another way, what is it that makes it possible for us to deal with people and love them?

_____

_____

_____

How does the religious expert try to test Jesus further?

_____

_____

_____

_____

_____

Jesus responded to the question of who is our neighbor by telling the story we now know as the Good Samaritan.

What contemporary religious comparison could we use to describe the vocation or function of the priest and temple assistant who passed by and failed to help the beaten man?

_____

_____

_____

_____

_____

Of course, the hero of the story who comes by, has compassion for the plight of the man, and takes care of him is a Samaritan. Why did the Jews hate Samaritans so much?

_____

_____

_____

_____

_____

I used a modern-day example of a Republican and Democrat passing the Samaritan by and a Communist helping the man. Can you think of another contemporary example that would have expressed this same principle?

_____

_____

_____

_____

_____

When the religious leader was forced to respond to Jesus' question as to who was his neighbor (remember, the religious leader had proposed this line of thought in the first place), he responded by saying it was the one who showed mercy. He couldn't even bring himself to use the word "Samaritan." Not only did the religious leader fail to trap Jesus into saying something contrary to the Torah, he also ended up with Jesus telling him that he should act like a hated Samaritan.

Is there some people group that you don't like or don't trust? Take a few minutes to consider why that might be the case. Were you conditioned that way by your parents or by some experiences? Explain.

_____

_____

_____

_____

_____

The most prevalent spirit of division in the United States is racism, which can come in different forms. It can be found both inside and outside the Church. What is the *only* way to defeat this spirit of division—to enable you to genuinely love people you would normally despise?

_____

_____

_____

_____

_____

WHEN WE LOVE GOD, WE CAN LOVE PEOPLE

Some people who love God claim not to be a "people person." Is it really possible to love God and keep His commandments and not love people? Explain.

_____

_____

_____

_____

_____

For most of us, there are even people in our own families that we would despise were it not for the love of God. But Jesus made clear that obeying these two commands is what will enable you to live your best life and to *enjoy* life. That means putting these principles into practice.

What will be the result of gaining financial success or fame if you are still mad at everybody you meet?

_____

_____

_____

_____

If you don't love God, you won't love people, and if you don't love people, you can't upset them. How do you respond to this principle?

_____

_____

_____

_____

What is a natural byproduct of loving God when it comes to relating to other people?

_____

_____

_____

_____

When you start becoming nicer and kinder, it is a result of being what?

_____

_____

_____

_____

Not being free doesn't mean that you are bound in sin. What happens when you are not totally free from where you came?

_____

_____

_____

_____

Read Proverbs 11:30 and Proverbs 16:7. What are the results of acting kindly (with mercy) and loving God, and having that love for God overflow to our everyday relationships even with those who are our enemies?

_____

_____

_____

_____

Read John 8:31. When we love God, what do we become faithful to in addition to Him?

_____

_____

_____

_____

Jesus upsets people wherever He goes. That was true 2,000 years ago, and it is true today. Jesus' disciples didn't always agree with everything He told them. However, they were ultimately recognized as His disciples because they were willing to do what He said, even if it didn't make sense at the time.

Describe a time when you obeyed what the Lord told you even though you didn't understand or even agree with it. Discuss.

_____

_____

_____

_____

I described a situation a few years ago where an LGBTQ group had planned to come to our church to protest. We prepared to offer refreshments and also had umbrellas on hand if the rain persisted. Even though they didn't show up that day, we were ready for them.

What principle did God use that situation to show us we had gotten backwards?

_____

_____

_____

_____

Respond to this statement: The truth is it's hard to hate up close: You have to be far away to hate.

_____

_____

_____

_____

While that group did not come to protest that day, there have since been others, and we have always greeted them with refreshments, cold bottles of water, hot cups of coffee, and lots of love and plenty of hugs.

Proverbs 25:21–22 is a foundational Scripture of this book:

> If your enemies are hungry, give them food to eat.
>> If they are thirsty, give them water to drink.
> You will heap burning coals of shame on their heads,
>> and the Lord will reward you.

In being taught to provide for our enemies, God says we will heap burning coals on their heads. Psalm 112:10 says that when we treat people who come against us with kindness and love, "The wicked will see this and be infuriated." Explain how showing God's love infuriates—upsets—people.

_____

_____

_____

_____

_____

I have three aunts who are lesbians. When I was growing up, one of them in particular was always very nice, kind, and encouraging to me. It wasn't until I was about 20 years old that I even found out she was in a relationship with other another woman. I love her, as I love all my aunts. I just don't agree with their lifestyle.

Loving like Christ loved means loving people in spite of our differences. We, as the body of Christ, can't just walk past people who are broken and hurting. If you can't love people right where they are, you probably have a hard time receiving love from God. The truth is, hurt people hurt people. But the good news is that free people free people, and upset people upset people.

If you allow a religious perspective into your heart, who are you likely to love or not love? Why?

_____

_____

_____

_____

What is your experience dealing with others who, like my aunts, have lifestyles or are in relationships that are clearly not Christlike? How should you interact with them? How should the local church relate to them?

_____

_____

_____

_____

Activation:

- Think of a person who would be your equivalent of the Samaritan. Ask God to remove anything that would keep you from genuinely loving this person.
- Choose a difficult person to "go after" in prayer this week.

CHAPTER 3
UPSETTERS NEED THE HOLY SPIRIT

God, thank You for sending the Holy Spirit to upset me. Amen.

Key Scriptures: John 14:15–17; Romans 8:11; John 16:8, 13

Back in the early 2000s, an MTV show that documented a celebrity's life and was narrated by the celebrity always began the story with, "You think you know ... but you have no idea." Based upon what many of us have heard about the Holy Spirit, I think He might say that same thing to us today.

The Holy Spirit is God, and He's not just a side person in the Trinity. He is equal to and as vital as God the Father and God the Son. Like God the Father and God the Son, the Holy Spirit is a *person*, not some crazy ghostly power.

What were you taught about the Holy Spirit when you were taught about God?

_____

_____

_____

_____

_____

Why do you think so many people are misinformed about the Holy Spirit?

_____

_____

_____

_____

_____

HE LEADS US INTO TRUTH

The Holy Spirit came to lead us into the truth. Truth isn't a philosophy or ideology. ***Truth is a person, and His name is Jesus***.

How does Jesus describe His nature and character in John 14:6?

_____

_____

_____

_____

It is only the work of the Holy Spirit that brings people to Jesus. Jesus took something as simple as communicating the gospel and decided to use that, along with the Holy Spirit's power, to bring people to Him. God uses us as vessels of that Spirit. The Spirit is the one doing the work.

Even the apostle Paul calls preaching "foolishness" (see 1 Corinthians 1:17–18). He is saying that, like many other things, just using words to communicate the gospel shouldn't work. This is just one of many things God uses to further His kingdom that, in our human eyes, seem foolish and shouldn't work.

What are some of the examples of things God used for His purposes that by man's reasoning should not work?

_____

_____

_____

_____

All of these things and events help accomplish God's purposes because the Holy Spirit is at work in the background.

HE TEACHES AND REMINDS US

But when the Father sends the Advocate as my representative—that is, the Holy Spirit—he will teach you everything and will remind you of everything I have told you (John 14:26).

The reason we have the Gospels today is because the Holy Spirit reminded Matthew, Mark, Luke, and John of everything that happened during the time they spent with Jesus during His ministry.

How does the Holy Spirit remind us today of the things Jesus said?

_____

_____

_____

_____

Have you ever had the experience of not being able to choose the right words in speaking to someone about Jesus? Explain.

_____

_____

_____

_____

Why is it so important to read the Bible every day?

_____

_____

_____

_____

How can you tell the difference between people who want the power of the Holy Spirit but not the person?

_____

_____

_____

_____

If we are to be upsetters, how should our character and actions reflect the nature and personality of the Holy Spirit?

_____

_____

_____

_____

HE TESTIFIES

The Holy Spirit testifies about Jesus, and He can do that because He was and is with Him. Romans 8:11 tells us, "The Spirit of God, who raised Jesus from the dead, lives in you."

What are some of the things about Jesus that the Holy Spirit testifies?

_____

_____

_____

_____

_____

Jesus could only do the things He did on earth because He was filled with the Holy Spirit. He was filled with the Spirit when He was in His mother's womb, but because He was in a human body, He was limited to the same parameters we're limited to. Jesus depended on the Holy Spirit to do the powerful and miraculous things during His earthly ministry.

Read John 14:15–17. How did the power the disciples were able to display change once the Holy Spirit *indwelled* them?

_____

_____

_____

_____

_____

In the same way Jesus needed the Holy Spirit, we need Him to go with us in order for us to upset the world.

HE CONVICTS PEOPLE OF SIN

God sent the Holy Spirit to represent Christ's interest on earth. As our Advocate, the Holy Spirit is like a lawyer who gives us counsel and protects our interests.

How does the Holy Spirit protect Jesus' followers?

_____

_____

_____

_____

When the disciples went out to upset the world after Jesus ascended to heaven, the Holy Spirit was with them and gave them words to say. In the same way, He comes to us today to testify about the Father and Jesus and give us the right and the ability to speak as diplomatic citizens of heaven.

According to Romans 10:9, what is the importance and result of our speaking and confessing Jesus with our mouth? (See Luke 6:45 NKJV).

_____

_____

_____

_____

Jesus makes it clear in John 16:8 that it is the Holy Spirit who will convict the world of its sin. It won't be me drawing up a list of all the sins you can do and making you feel bad about it.

I related a story about the Holy Spirit convicting one of our members about his immoral lifestyle while I was preaching about giving. Describe how you feel the Holy Spirit was working in that situation.

_____

_____

_____

_____

_____

The Holy Spirit continues to convict us of sin even after we're saved. The Holy Spirit shows people the real nature of their sin, the truth about righteousness found only in God, and the coming judgment.

If we are praying for a loved one, what should we do rather than just confront them?

_____

_____

_____

_____

_____

HE TELLS US WHAT JESUS IS SAYING NOW

When the Spirit of truth comes, he will guide you into all truth. He will not speak on his own but will tell you what he has heard. He will tell you about the future. He will bring me glory by telling you whatever he receives from me. All that belongs to the Father is mine; this is why I said, "The Spirit will tell you whatever he receives from me" (John 16:13–15).

This passage deals with more than just prophecy. Many people show up to church expecting to hear a word to help them get a breakthrough in their life.

What does "the future" mean in this passage?

_____

_____

_____

_____

What is the role of a preacher or pastor in the church assembly?

_____

_____

_____

_____

Do you think some people become too reliant upon pastors, preachers, or teachers to hear from the Holy Spirit? Explain.

_____

_____

_____

_____

How do you imagine that God, Jesus, and the Holy Spirit communicate with each other in helping guide their children?

_____

_____

_____

_____

I relate the story of how I argued with the Holy Spirit about asking for the smaller, more affordable apartment when I moved from California to Texas. Why did I feel like I had to ignore His advice and continue with the paperwork for the larger apartment?

_____

_____

_____

_____

Have you ever argued with or resisted the voice of the Holy Spirit? Describe the experience and the results.

_____

_____

_____

_____

Maybe you need Jesus to bend down and whisper in the Holy Spirit's ear about a situation in your life. Maybe it's something you're going through with a friend or a co-worker. Maybe you need Him to tell you how to reach the person who refuses to go to church with you. Maybe you need Him to tell you who He wants you to upset with His gospel message. Whatever it is, He's ready and willing to speak to you about what's going on in your life right now.

What is going on in your life right now that you could use advice or help from God with? What are you going to do about it?

_____

_____

_____

_____

Activation

- What does it mean to you to look and act like the Holy Spirit?
- If you need a word from the Lord, ask the Holy Spirit today. He wants to speak to you.

CHAPTER 4
UPSETTERS AREN'T IN CONTROL

Holy Spirit, I submit my will to Yours. Change me. Amen.

Key Scriptures: Acts 19:3-4; Ephesians 5:18; Galatians 5:22-23

We already learned that we need the Holy Spirit if we're going to upset the world, but you need to know *why* you need Him. You need to know who He is and what He does, because if you haven't been Spirit-filled, you may feel a little bit like I did when I first got saved.

Describe an experience where someone tried strongly to convince you of something without explaining it to you. How did that make you feel?

_____

_____

_____

_____

_____

Scripture is very clear that when someone gives their life to Jesus, it's because the Holy Spirit *brought* them to Jesus. However, Scripture is also clear that Jesus has reserved the right to baptize people *into* the Holy Spirit. These are two very different things.

> If you love me, obey my commandments. And I will ask the Father, and he will give you another Advocate, who will never leave you. He is the Holy Spirit, who leads into all truth. The world cannot receive him, because it isn't looking for him and doesn't recognize him. But

you know him, because **he lives with you now and later will be in you** (John 14:15–17, emphasis added).

Explain what it means that the Holy Spirit can be *with* you but not *in* you.

_____

_____

_____

_____

_____

In the nineteenth chapter of Acts we read about this very situation. Paul asks the saints in Ephesus if they had received the Holy Spirit when they believed. Now, if they had already received Jesus, shouldn't they already have the Holy Spirit? Paul is clearly asking this question because the Holy Spirit can be *with* you but not *in* you.

Many people in churches today would answer as those in Ephesus did. They have learned about God the Father and God the Son, but the Holy Spirit has often been avoided in their church. Being filled with the Spirit is sometimes associated with wild or crazy experiences.

What was your first introduction to the Holy Spirit?

_____

_____

_____

_____

_____

Read Acts 19:3–4. Into which baptism did those Ephesian disciples say they had been baptized? How did Paul explain that baptism to them?

_____

_____

_____

_____

Read Acts 19:5–7. What did Paul do to those disciples and how did they respond?

_____

_____

_____

_____

In this passage, how many disciples were baptized into the Holy Spirit? What, if any, significance do you attach to that number? Explain.

_____

_____

_____

_____

They believed in Jesus—they were Christians—but they were not Spirit-filled. Then Paul prayed for them, the Holy Spirit came on them, and they were filled. That word _on_ can also mean _in_. They were in-filled with, or baptized in, the Holy Spirit, and this is Jesus' assignment for all of us as upsetters.

What are the four passages, one from each of the gospels, that speak of baptism in the Holy Spirit?

_____

_____

_____

_____

How many witnesses are typically required for agreement of a testimony?

_____

_____

_____

_____

Once you understand who the Holy Spirit is and what He does, all fear and anxiety about Him will be eliminated. Scripture is very clear, especially in the book of Proverbs, that it's important to have understanding. Besides Proverbs 3:13 and 8:9, what are a few passages that speak of the need for understanding?

_____

_____

_____

_____

The simple truth is that if the people telling me about the Holy Spirit when I first got saved had an understanding and could have explained why I needed to be filled with Him, I wouldn't have felt like they were forcing Him on me. If we're going to upset the world, it's important not only to understand why we need the infilling of the Holy Spirit, but we also need to be able to explain Him to others and tell them why they need to be filled with Him too.

Explain in your own words why it is important to be filled with the Holy Spirit.

_____

_____

_____

_____

UPSETTERS NEED TO BE FILLED

Ephesians 5:18 says, "Don't be drunk with wine, because that will ruin your life. Instead, be filled with the Holy Spirit."

At first glance, it's shocking to think that this comparative analysis to being filled with the Holy Spirit is getting drunk with wine. But the reason he uses this is that alcohol has a counterfeit effect on your life, in your body, and in your system from that of the Holy Spirit. What Paul is actually saying is, "You don't have to do it *that* way. You can do it *this* way. Don't get drunk with wine. Get drunk with something good—the Holy Spirit."

What are the eight brief definitions of filled?

_____

_____

_____

_____

The Holy Spirit fills us—the receptacles—to full capacity and an extreme degree, satisfying us fully by being plentiful throughout and pervading completely. What is the other, perhaps most important thing, that the Holy Spirit does when we are filled with Him?

_____

_____

_____

_____

_____

If you consumed an entire bottle of vodka, you would change, even if you tried your best not to. The spirit in the bottle of vodka will change you. It changes the way you walk. It changes your character.

Being filled with the Holy Spirit also changes the way you walk. Here's what Paul was saying to us: "Don't get drunk with that spirit. Get drunk with the Holy Spirit. He can do the same thing the spirit in the bottle can do, except He does it in a completely opposite way. You won't walk crooked; you'll actually walk straight. You'll be a different person if you let the Holy Spirit fill you. You've been trying to walk on your own, and you get kind of sideways and can't stay on the line, but don't worry! We all miss the mark, and I understand that. But if you live your life Spirit-filled and Spirit-led, you will be walking in a straight line. And when you start to get off the line, the Holy Spirit will say, 'Hey, you're off the line,' and will gently guide you back."

What are some examples of where you may have been starting to walk "off the line" in your life, but the Holy Spirit brought you back?

_____

_____

_____

_____

If you are filled with vodka, your speech will change. Being filled with the Spirit also changes the way you talk. It changes your conversation. I grew up in a Pentecostal church that was very charismatic. When I talk about the Holy Spirit changing the way you talk, the first thing most people with a background similar to mine think about is speaking in tongues. But that's not what I'm talking about. I'm not talking about a prayer language, or the gift of tongues (1 Corinthians 13:1). I'm not even talking about a heavenly language where the Holy Spirit prays for you (Romans 8:26–27). I'm literally talking about your conversations with people. The things you talk about with other people change when you're filled with the Holy Spirit.

If you've been filled with the Holy Spirit, how did the things you talk about change after your experience? If not, what changes have you noticed in family or friends who have been filled with the Holy Spirit?

_____

_____

_____

_____

How is the Holy Spirit like a "quality assurance" check on what comes out of your mouth?

_____

_____

_____

_____

Read Proverbs 18:21 and James 3:9–10. What do these passages teach us about the importance of what we say?

_____

_____

_____

_____

How does Galatians 5:22–23 teach us about what it looks like to be Spirit-filled?

_____

_____

_____

_____

Acts 2 is when the Holy Spirit fell, but by Acts 4, the believers were asking for refills. I don't know if it was 3 days or 7 days or 14 days, but they couldn't go a couple of weeks without needing a refill of the Holy Spirit to give them what they needed to go back out and declare Jesus Christ with boldness.

Why is it important for us, as believers and upsetters, to be continually refilled with the Holy Spirit?

_____

_____

_____

_____

Being filled with a spirit can change the way people act. For example, sometimes a normally docile person will become bolder when they have been drinking. The way they act when they're filled with the spirit is very different from how they conduct themselves in their everyday lives.

The same is true for us when we're filled with the Holy Spirit. When the Holy Spirit is in you, it makes it difficult to walk away from your relationship with Jesus, because He's there *with* you.

How might—or has—the enemy tried to lure you away with a temptation of a negative thought?

_____

_____

_____

_____

How does the Holy Spirit help us respond to those temptations?

_____

_____

_____

_____

Describe a time, either from your own life or that of someone you are close to, where you or they went back to an old lifestyle after once turning away from it.

_____

_____

_____

_____

How does the behavior of the disciples in John 21 show that they had not yet been filled with the Spirit?

_____

_____

_____

_____

Read Acts 4:1–22. How does the response of the disciples to Annas and Caiaphas in verses 7–10 demonstrate their being filled with the Spirit?

_____

_____

_____

_____

What does Romans 8:11 say about the indwelling of the Spirit?

_____

_____

_____

_____

If we're going to be upsetters, we need to get used to not being in control. When someone is drunk with a spirit, they're *not* in control, and the spirit makes them do crazy things. In the same way, when someone is filled with the Holy Spirit, they're not in control, and the Spirit makes them do crazy *and* amazing things! Things they could never have done without Him.

What crazy things have you seen done by someone who is drunk with alcohol or drugs?

_____

_____

_____

_____

What are some amazing things that you have seen done through the work of the Holy Spirit?

_____

_____

_____

_____

Why is wine a cheap imitation of the Holy Spirit? What things will you see changed in your life if you let Him fill you completely?

_____

_____

_____

_____

You don't have to wait for a church service or for someone to come to your house and pray with you. Jesus wants to give you the gift of the Holy Spirit right now. All you have to do is have an open heart to receive Him. It's that simple.

Activation:

- If you've never been filled with the Holy Spirit, ask Jesus to baptize you in the Holy Spirit today.
- If you need a "refill" of the Holy Spirit, don't be afraid to ask. We all need a *daily* portion of the Holy Spirit.

CHAPTER 5
UPSETTERS AREN'T RELIGIOUS

Lord, help me not to be a religious hypocrite. Amen.

Key Scriptures: Philippians 2:3–5; Matthew 11:28–30

I hadn't been saved 90 days when I started attending a Bible study at a new church. At the beginning of the meeting, everyone went around the room and shared a little bit about themselves. I told the group how excited I was because I had just gotten saved! The leader looked at me and said, "Do you speak in tongues? Because if you don't speak in tongues, you're not really saved."

This leader said the same thing about the grandmother of one of the other guys in the group. This comment really bothered me. However, when I asked my momma about this, she made it clear that speaking in tongues was not a requirement for my salvation.

Have you ever been told something by a leader or teacher that just didn't seem correct or scriptural to you? What did you do? Explain.

_____

_____

_____

_____

Why do some people believe that speaking in tongues is required in order to be saved? What do you think about that?

_____

_____

_____

_____

What is salvation based on?

_____

_____

_____

_____

RELIGION VS. RELATIONSHIP

There's been a lot of talk over the last decade about religion versus relationship. I've heard many people say, "I don't want anything to do with religion. I just want a relationship with Jesus." I understand what they're trying to communicate, but the truth of the matter is we're all religious. There's nothing inherently wrong with religion. In fact, most of us have some religious proclivities.

What kinds of things, related to faith and church, are you religious about (do you do religiously)?

_____

_____

_____

_____

What kinds of things, not related to faith and church, are you religious about?

_____

_____

_____

_____

The problem comes in when religion is what motivates us. We need to ask ourselves: *Are we being motivated to serve the Lord by religion? Or are we being motivated by our relationship with Jesus Christ?*

In Matthew 23:1–36, Jesus is talking to the crowds and His disciples, but He's really calling out the religious leaders and exposing their hypocrisy. He's telling the people to obey their instructions, but not their behavior.

What was the basic problem Jesus had with the behavior of these religious leaders, as He described in vv. 3–4?

_____

_____

_____

_____

_____

Is there any problem with formal liturgies and accepted conventions of behavior such as men wearing a suit and tie or women wearing a hat to church? Why or why not?

_____

_____

_____

_____

_____

It's the *heart behind* what you're doing that indicates if you have a religious spirit or not. And here's what Jesus is saying in the most scathing way: "Religion doesn't work."

What kinds of things did the Pharisees do to demonstrate their education, faith, and adherence to the law?

_____

_____

_____

_____

How did the Pharisees want themselves to be viewed?

_____

_____

_____

_____

It's not uncommon for some high priests and rabbis to wear tefillin today. It's not only worn to serve as a "sign" and "remembrance" that God brought the children of Israel out of Egypt but also because they are still religious and living by the law of the Old Testament. They're bound to religion. Their motivation for wearing it is out of fear of breaking the law, instead of being motivated by a relationship with Jesus.

What do you think of the practice of getting Scriptures tattooed on one's body? Have you had that done or know people who have? What should be the motivation behind having that done?

_____

_____

_____

_____

What does the example from Acts 19, where the seven sons of Sceva went around casting out evil spirits in the name of the Lord, teach about the power of one's name—and specifically the name of Jesus?

_____

_____

_____

_____

If you think looking and acting like you're religious is going to bring you into some type of special relationship with God, you have severely disconnected yourself from the Christ who came to redeem the law taught by these religious people. Religion isn't Jesus, and Jesus isn't religion. In fact, when you're acting religious, you don't look or act like Jesus.

Why don't you look like Jesus when you are acting religious?

_____

_____

_____

_____

When Jesus was on earth in His earthly body, how did He look in appearance compared to His disciples and others around Him?

_____

_____

_____

_____

Philippians 2:3–5 says, "Don't be selfish; don't try to impress others. Be humble, thinking of others as better than yourselves. Don't look out only for your own interests, but take an interest in others, too. You must have the same attitude that Christ Jesus had."

Why is this passage a perfect description of how an upsetter should look?

_____

_____

_____

_____

What are some of the titles the Bible uses to describe Jesus?

_____

_____

_____

_____

Do these titles have any power according to Scripture? Why or why not?

_____

_____

_____

_____

Angels bow in reverence to *His name*, and everyone on earth will too. *His name*, not His title, has power. And because we have a relationship with Him, we have that same power.

Describe in what ways we share the power of Jesus when we have a relationship with Him.

_____

_____

_____

_____

_____

Read Matthew 23:13–14. What was the word Jesus used over and over again to describe the Pharisees and other religious teachers? What was the consequence of the religious leaders placing harsh restrictions on the people in the name of religion?

_____

_____

_____

_____

_____

According to Matthew 5:17–20, how does Jesus describe His mission on earth relative to the law of Moses and the prophets?

_____

_____

_____

_____

_____

What does Jesus mean when He says that a person's righteousness must be greater than the righteousness of the Pharisees in order to enter the kingdom of heaven?

_____

_____

_____

_____

Describe the process of how a changed heart leads to changed behavior.

_____

_____

_____

_____

What are some of the things religious people say to us?

_____

_____

_____

_____

What criticisms or demands about your behavior have you personally experienced? How did you respond?

_____

_____

_____

_____

Six months after I got saved, I was baptized in the Holy Spirit. There wasn't a prayer revival, and I didn't have to follow any rules or be in a certain place doing a certain thing. This beautiful language started flowing out of my mouth. My mind didn't go blank, my eyes didn't roll in the back of my head, and I wasn't scared. For 20 minutes I prayed in this language. I knew it wasn't gibberish; there was structure and syntax to it. It was beautiful! And I didn't have to use a checklist to make sure I was doing everything the "right" way. I received my prayer language, and it was amazingly easy and fantastic. *No deep, religious experience necessary.*

If you have been baptized in the Holy Spirit, what was your experience?

_____

_____

_____

_____

_____

If you speak in tongues, how did you receive the gift, and what is your experience with it?

_____

_____

_____

_____

_____

Is it absolutely necessary that you be in church every Sunday or whenever the doors are opened? Why or why not?

_____

_____

_____

_____

_____

Read Matthew 11:28–30. What does it mean to let Jesus carry our burdens?

_____

_____

_____

_____

_____

What does it mean to you, personally, to let Jesus carry *your* burdens? What burden is He asking you to hand over to Him *right now*?

_____

_____

_____

_____

_____

RELIGION = RULES, BUT JESUS = GRACE

My father-in-law received Jesus and was saved while on his deathbed. Some people would say that he would have had to recite the sinner's prayer in order to be saved. What have you been taught about the process of salvation and what is required? Is it a "religious" process?

_____

_____

_____

_____

How did Juliette's and my experience at the Gateway presbytery service confirm the validity of my father-in-law's salvation?

_____

_____

_____

_____

Read Mark 12:26–27. What does it mean to you that "God is the God of the living, not the dead"?

_____

_____

_____

_____

Religion tries to make us think we have to wait until Sunday or be in a church building or have everything right in our lives in order to be saved. But that's not what the Bible says. The Bible says Jesus will never reject those who come to Him (John 6:37). It doesn't say we have to have everything together. We don't have to be perfect. We just have to come to Him, right where we are. Religion would make us think we have to follow certain rules or rituals before we come to Him. This is just another reason why Jesus hates religion.

What are some ways you will try to remove or overcome any religious spirit that you have in you today?

_____

_____

_____

_____

_____

Activation

- Ask the Lord, "Do I have a religious spirit about anything in my life?"
- Make sure the spiritual food you are consuming is "good food."

Holy Spirit, help me do good so I can upset people. Amen.

Key Scriptures: Acts 10:38; Galatians 6:9–10; Romans 2:7

Sometimes we set out to do something good, but it doesn't turn out exactly as expected. A couple years ago Joshua Brown with Daystar Television Network called me to arrange a campaign to bring a large amount of supplies to our church that we could then deliver to the homeless in Dallas. We loaded up several large SUV's with all kinds of supplies a homeless person might need and headed downtown to deliver them. But there was one problem. When we got there, we couldn't find anyone to help!

It was one of the coldest days of the year. We hunted for people for five hours before we realized that because of the cold, the police had gathered up the homeless and taken them off the streets. They brought them to shelters and even put some in jail to help them keep warm.

How much time had we set aside for this effort initially?

_____

_____

_____

_____

_____

What was our first reaction to not being able to find any recipients for these supplies? What did we end up doing instead?

_____

_____

_____

_____

_____

When we finally encountered the first two homeless men, what was the man's reply when I asked him how he had survived on the streets for nine years?

_____

_____

_____

_____

_____

There's a verse in the Bible that summarizes this perspective beautifully: "So don't worry about tomorrow, for tomorrow will bring its own worries. Today's trouble is enough for today" (Matthew 6:34). This homeless man made me look through the lens of my bougie, suburban perspective and think, *Why am I worrying about anything? Why am I letting my bills drive me crazy? Why am I allowing that situation at work to ruin my day?* The realization that this guy had survived nine years on the street by living out this principle reminded me that this is how we all need to be living our lives. One day at a time. No one is promised tomorrow. We need to do good *today*.

How do you tend to look at things when troubles or challenges arise? Are you focused on the future or content to let today's troubles be sufficient for the day? Explain and give an example.

_____

_____

_____

_____

When you give someone cash, do you think it is right to put stipulations on what they can do with the money? Why or why not?

_____

_____

_____

_____

Eventually we went back to where the homeless usually hang out. The shelters had been emptied, and we found more people back on the streets than we could possibly provide for. However, even those who we could not help, for the most part, were grateful for what we were doing.

What was—and is—the unintended incredible effect of being a blessing to someone?

_____

_____

_____

_____

FOLLOWING THE LEADER

If you want to know the whole formula for upsetting the world, it's right here in Acts 10:38: "And you know that God anointed Jesus of Nazareth with the Holy Spirit and with power. Then Jesus went around **doing good** and healing all who were oppressed by the devil, for God was with him" (emphasis added).

Why do you think people often skip over the part of this verse about Jesus doing good?

_____

_____

_____

_____

What is the sequence we need to follow based on this verse?

_____

_____

_____

_____

We have the same power Jesus had to cast out demons. But before He healed people who were demon-possessed, He went around *doing good*. **You want to know how to upset the world?** ***Do good.*** We live in a *very* cynical world. Do you know what can make a demon run faster than pouring out some oil? Being nice. You want to upset someone? Be nice and do something good for them.

When it comes to doing good works or using the power of Jesus to do miracles and cast out demons, which is most important? Which should we emphasize?

_____

_____

_____

_____

One of the rights we have as citizens of heaven is to be empowered by the Holy Spirit to take authority over spiritual wickedness in high places—the principalities in this world—but *not* at the expense of doing good. We shouldn't be so focused on this that we forget to do good things.

Describe the first miracle Jesus did at the wedding reception at Cana in Galilee. Why do you think Jesus chose this relatively simple and nondescript way to begin demonstrating His power?

_____

_____

_____

_____

John 2:11 says, "This miraculous sign at Cana in Galilee was the first time Jesus revealed his glory. And his disciples believed in him." What is the result of people seeing believers doing good things?

_____

_____

_____

_____

Jesus never stopped doing good things. Sometime later Jesus was out preaching on a hillside (see Matthew 14:13–21). About how many people in total were there on the hill listening to Jesus that day?

_____

_____

_____

_____

_____

Describe how you think the disciples felt when Jesus announced they were going to feed all those people? What limited amount of fish and bread did Andrew find to bring to Jesus?

_____

_____

_____

_____

_____

Describe in your own words the feeding of the crowds and how you think people reacted.

_____

_____

_____

_____

_____

Describe the other two examples of Jesus doing good in the text.

_____

_____

_____

_____

_____

When you're genuinely nice and do good things, you're being like Jesus, and like Him, you're going to upset people. The apostle Paul told believers,

> So let's not get tired of doing what is good. At just the right time we will reap a harvest of blessing if we don't give up. Therefore, whenever we have the opportunity, we should do good to everyone—especially to those in the family of faith (Galatians 6:9–10).

Are you an outgoing people-person or are you hesitant and standoffish around people you don't know? How should you look once Jesus has taken His place in your life?

_____

_____

_____

_____

_____

Are there some boundary lines you have placed as to where Jesus can have access to your life? If so, what are these limits to His lordship, and what will you do to remove those boundaries?

_____

_____

_____

_____

_____

IT'S WHO WE ARE

Upsetters do good *all the time*. This should be our lifestyle and how we go about our everyday lives. Romans 2:7 says, "He will give eternal life to those who keep on doing good, seeking after the glory and honor and immortality that God offers."

How do you feel about the idea that this verse approves and encourages the believer to seek after glory and honor and immortality? Does that sound greedy or selfish to you? Explain.

_____

_____

_____

_____

_____

What is the simple way to start doing what Romans 2:7 teaches?

_____

_____

_____

_____

_____

How profound an impact might you have on a person's life just by doing something good for them?

_____

_____

_____

_____

_____

Things won't always go the way you plan. We didn't plan to drive to Dallas and not find one single person we could bless. It's important for us to remember what Proverbs 16:9 says:

> We can make our plans,
>   but the Lord determines our steps.

It's not up to us to decide who wants to be upset or who doesn't. It's just our assignment to upset. If we're going to upset the world, we have to do good deeds.

Describe a time when some effort you made to help or do something for someone turned out differently than you had planned. What was the result and the lesson learned from that experience?

_____

_____

_____

_____

I named this book *Upset the World* because we *all* have a world. You have your home life world, you have your work world, and you have your fun, play world. Whatever world you're in, go upset it in the name of Jesus Christ.

What will happen in people's lives when you do good things, whether or not you do any of the "big stuff" that typically gets celebrated in church?

_____

_____

_____

_____

How will you ask God to empower you to be like Jesus in doing good?

_____

_____

_____

_____

If we all commit to doing good, we *will* upset the world.

Activation

- Read about Jesus' good deeds in the Gospel of Matthew.
- Ask God whom you should upset this week with your good deeds.

CHAPTER 7
UPSETTERS LOVE LIFE

Holy Spirit, give me a joy that will upset the world. Amen.

Key Scriptures: Nehemiah 8:10; Ephesians 5:2; Psalm 30:11–12

For the majority of my life I have been an expressive and joyful person. It's how God created me, and my mom would tell you that I've been that way from the time I was born.

However, that joyful nature was repressed after I was molested when I was eight years old by a neighbor who lived across the street. It was traumatic. I maintained a happy outward persona because I was terrified that my parents would find out. I carried that dark secret deep inside.

What was the big reason I was afraid to tell my dad what had happened?

_____

_____

_____

_____

_____

Have you or someone you know had a traumatic experience as a young child that was repressed? What were the circumstances?

_____

_____

_____

_____

_____

This situation led to me also lying about my life. I had to say that everything was okay when it really wasn't. I forced myself to be happy. I was still an outwardly expressive person, but I was putting on a show so no one would see the truth. I began to play a role as the "happy and funny boy" so people wouldn't ask me what was wrong. I also had trouble at school, and my grades suffered as a result.

What were your childhood fears? Were they rational or irrational?

_____

_____

_____

_____

Was there a time when you were young that, either because of a traumatic experience or because of fear, your behavior changed? Explain.

_____

_____

_____

_____

At the age of 12 I was exposed to pornography, and it became my drug. It was exhilarating, and it took my mind off of other, less pleasant situations. By the age of 19 I was a full-blown porn-addict. It was ruling my life. I knew in my heart what I was doing was wrong, but like any addiction, it had a tight hold on me. I couldn't stop even though I wanted to.

Why is addiction so isolating?

_____

_____

_____

_____

_____

Why do you think many young people, in particular, begin to engage in addictive behavior?

_____

_____

_____

_____

_____

Was there something that you, or perhaps a sibling, were addicted to as a young person, even if it was just some form of electronic device? What was the effect?

_____

_____

_____

_____

_____

When I was 19 years old, I got caught by my mom. It was 2 a.m., and I was watching porn on our big screen television in the back of the house. I didn't hear her walking down the hall, and she walked right in on me and saw it all. It was *horrible*! I was mortified. Embarrassed. Sick. Devastated.

What was my mother's immediate reaction when she learned of my porn addiction early that morning? What does her reaction say about my mom's nature and relationship with God?

_____

_____

_____

_____

I decided to come clean about what I understood was the root cause of my addiction, so I told my momma about the molestation. Myles had also been molested by the same man. We also related to her how, when Myles and I were 14 and 15 years old, we went to our neighbor's house with serious thoughts of killing the neighbor, only to call it off when we realized the neighbor seemed to have no remembrance of what had happened.

What other influence do you believe may have been at work in my and Myles's lives when we walked away from that confrontation with the neighbor?

_____

_____

_____

_____

Momma called my dad and had him come home from his night job at the Post Office. At 4 a.m., Myles and I told him our stories, but what happened next took us by surprise. My mom told us she was sexually abused by her babysitters when she was six years old. And then my dad shared that he gotten molested by a comic book store owner when he was five years old. In one night, all the family secrets were out. It was over.

Share a time when you learned something shocking about the life of a relative or close friend. What was your reaction? What was the response or effect on the other person?

_____

_____

_____

_____

As we all shared that night, the bondage broke. I wasn't completely free of the addiction, but a light was put on it, and the frequency of the occurrences lessened because I was finally able to talk about it.

Why are addictions so isolating? What is the underlying reason that isolation exists and continues?

_____

_____

_____

_____

What does your body do if you can't express yourself and deal with your isolation verbally?

_____

_____

_____

_____

Six months later, I gave my life to Christ, and that's when the boulder was lifted and my new life began. That was the *only* thing that was holding me back. Nevertheless. it took over a decade of counseling because I wasn't satisfied with stopping the action. I wanted to get to the root. Then I had to deal with the question, "What made me get to the point where I wanted to murder someone?" That took about another decade of counseling.

Have you or someone you know had to undergo counseling to deal with abuse or a traumatic situation from their past? Why is it necessary and important to deal thoroughly with such events or experiences?

_____

_____

_____

_____

_____

THE JOY OF THE LORD

You may be thinking, *Why is Tim sharing this story in a chapter he titled "Upsetters Love Life"?* It's because the story I just shared with you could have *completely* ended my love for life. But it didn't. And if you have a similar story, it doesn't have to end yours either.

So many people allow the negative circumstances of their past to write negativity for every day of their present and future. I've known too many believers who are walking around with a victim mentality. The pain of your past is real, but how do you get over it? That cannot remain the narrative of your entire life.

Read Romans 6:6–7. How and why does Jesus want to bring freedom to any area of your life that is stealing your joy?

_____

_____

_____

_____

Why did I have to put my personal experience and testimony about abuse and porn to the side and not make it the focus of my preaching? How might you apply that concept to any similar situation in your life?

_____

_____

_____

_____

Upsetters have to love life in spite of the negative stuff that happens to them. You have to find where the joy is and ride it out. And where is the joy? It's found in the Lord. The Bible says, "Don't be dejected and sad, for the joy of the Lord is your strength!" (Nehemiah 8:10).

Before I gave my life to Jesus Christ, what I thought I loved about my life, I really didn't. I loved some parts of it. I loved some highlights of it, but I wasn't in love with my *entire* life. When I gave my life to Jesus and started following His example, I started to *love* the life I was living because I had a blueprint of how to *really* live it.

How is Ephesians 5:2 a blueprint for how we can love our life? Explain.

_____

_____

_____

_____

I don't like to preach motivational ideas just for the sake of being motivational. Who does motivation need to be empowered by in order to be more than just a pep talk?

_____

_____

_____

_____

Why does just thinking positive thoughts or having positive energy not lead to good things happening?

_____

_____

_____

_____

If we're going to live our lives as upsetters, it means we're going to love Jesus, love people, be spirit-filled, not be religious, do good, and *love life*. You—yes, *you*—can love life. Remember, the joy of the Lord is your strength. Joy that comes from the Lord is what lasts.

Look up several passages of Scripture that deal with the joy of the Lord. Write them here.

_____

_____

_____

_____

_____

There have been some incredibly dark moments in my life. I don't love those dark moments, but I still love my life. I love my life because it's been completely upset by Jesus Christ. He completely overturned *everything* I thought about life and gave me a proper perspective on it.

Yes, bad things will happen. Some days are good. Some days are bad. And some days are really bad.

One of the darkest days of my life was when I lost my brother. Myles had been my best friend for practically my whole life. He was killed in an automobile accident at the age of 27. Even though that day was dark, I still had the joy of the Lord. It truly was my strength. We can hold on to the promise that says,

> Weeping may last through the night,
>   but joy comes with the morning (Psalm 30:5).

A trait of being a believer is being joyful. We have the joy of the Lord. And it's something that upsets others. Our love of life and joy in the Lord will draw people to Him and upset their lives in the best possible way.

Share some examples from people you know who have responded with joy to pain and tragedy.

_____

_____

_____

_____

_____

What does Acts 13:49–52 tell us about the relationship of joy and the Holy Spirit and how we, as believers, respond to that joy?

_____

_____

_____

_____

_____

How has your relationship with Jesus Christ helped you break with the bondage of your past?

_____

_____

_____

_____

_____

It was the overwhelming love of Jesus Christ that turned my life upside down. He did it for me, and He can do it for you too.

Activation

- Don't allow the enemy to isolate you. Find one or two trustworthy friends with whom you can share your struggles.
- Memorize Scriptures about joy, such as Psalm 30:11–12. No matter what is going on in your life, you can choose to be joyful today.

CHAPTER 8
UPSETTERS DISTURB THE PIECE

Holy Spirit, help me disturb the piece so I can upset people.
Amen.

Key Scriptures: John 4:7; Matthew 8:14–15; Luke 19:9–10; Luke 23:33

As ambassadors of Christ, we've been commissioned to upset others by disturbing the piece of them that's not in harmony with Jesus Christ. If we're going to upset the world, it means we're going to interfere with and disarrange the piece in people's lives that's not in alignment with the Word of God.

What are some general ways that God might show up in our lives and disturb the piece?

_____

_____

_____

_____

What is a time you can remember that God disturbed a piece of your life? Explain.

_____

_____

_____

_____

We see it all throughout the Bible, but particularly in the Gospels. Jesus comes into people's lives, and suddenly, everything is turned upside down. Jesus often helps realign things in people's lives. But there are the times

Jesus chooses to come into our life and disturb the piece by addressing situations, thoughts, habits, and addictions. When He addresses the sin in our lives, He completely upsets us.

These four instances from Jesus' time on earth demonstrate where He _____ and _____ addressed the situation in someone's life, and He's the one who _____ it.

THE WOMAN

Read John 4:1–3. What was Jesus doing that got the attention of the Pharisees? Why did this prompt His decision to return to Galilee?

_____

_____

_____

_____

_____

Did Jesus *have* to go through Samaria on His way to Galilee? Why did He go that way? What was He *strategically* doing by choosing that route?

_____

_____

_____

_____

_____

Why was it unusual for Jesus to ask for a drink of water from the Samaritan woman? What does this show about His reason for selecting this woman to meet there?

_____

_____

_____

_____

_____

At what time of day did women normally go to the well to draw water? What was the likely reason that this woman was coming in the middle of the day?

_____

_____

_____

_____

_____

Why do you think Jesus came to approach the woman at this time of day?

_____

_____

_____

_____

_____

Why did the woman respond the way she did to Jesus telling her that if she drinks the water He has to offer, she would never be thirsty again? How did her background and circumstances feed into her answer?

_____

_____

_____

_____

What aspect or piece of the woman's life does Jesus' response in John 4:16 show that He is disturbing? Explain.

_____

_____

_____

_____

Jesus could have chastised her about her past behavior and current situation, but He does not. Instead, He lovingly and kindly addresses her instability. What is the woman's response to Jesus' words? Who does she tell and what does she tell all the people in the village?

_____

_____

_____

_____

The place He picks is Samaria, the person He picks is the woman at the well, and the piece of her life He disturbs is her instability.

THE MOTHER-IN-LAW

Matthew 8:14–15 relates the story of Jesus healing Peter's mother-in-law.

Do you think that Jesus went to Peter's house at Peter's request for the purpose of healing? Explain.

_____

_____

_____

_____

_____

Why do you think Jesus responded so quickly and simply to the situation He encountered?

Read the first 13 verses of Matthew 8. It contains two other examples of healing by Jesus, but under quite different circumstances.

What was different about the healing of the man with leprosy in verses 1–4? Who made the approach for healing, and what was the purpose of or lesson to be learned from the response Jesus requested of the leper?

_____

_____

_____

_____

_____

In verses 5–13, who approached whom for healing? What lessons about proximity and faith could be learned from this example? When, where, how, and why was the young servant healed?

_____

_____

_____

_____

_____

What are some of the thoughts or insecurities that might come to mind as reasons for us not to pray for someone when God prompts us to do so?

_____

_____

_____

_____

_____

Do you have to have someone's permission to pray for them? Do you need to be right there with that person to pray for them? Explain.

_____

_____

_____

_____

_____

Is it always necessary to lay hands on people who are sick and pray long dramatic prayers? When do you think laying on of hands might be appropriate or necessary? Explain.

_____

_____

_____

_____

What do you think God is looking at or considering about your prayers when He responds?

_____

_____

_____

_____

What is a "Father God" prayer? How do you feel about such prayers?

_____

_____

_____

_____

All Jesus wants from us is to be obedient and to pray for people when He leads us, and He'll do the rest. We don't have to worry about how long we pray or how it sounds; we just need to be willing to disturb their piece.

The place He picks is Peter's house, the person He picks is Peter's mother-in-law, and the piece of her life He disturbs is her sickness.

THE TAX COLLECTOR

Read the story of Zacchaeus in Luke 19:1–10.

Why did Zacchaeus go ahead on Jesus' planned route and climb the sycamore-fig tree? What is the difference between the common fig tree and the sycamore-fig tree? How difficult do you think it was to climb?

_____

_____

_____

_____

We don't read anything of Zacchaeus prior to this brief story. What do you think may have been in Zacchaeus's mind that prompted his unusual efforts to see Jesus?

_____

_____

_____

_____

Did Jesus ask anything of Zacchaeus (as far as we read) that prompted his offer to give away his wealth and compensate people he had cheated?

_____

_____

_____

_____

Like Zacchaeus, there are a lot of people in this world who are rich by the world's standards, but their identities are in their success. When your identity is found in your success, you're really covering up something on the inside of you that feels rejected. You turn to your vocation or your bank account or your degrees on the wall to affirm you, but those things will *never* affirm you like the One who created you. God not only affirms you, but He also fills you with His joy and peace (Romans 15:13). Jesus decided to disturb the piece of rejection that was in Zacchaeus's heart.

When Zacchaeus offered to give back four times what he had cheated people, he was going above and beyond what the Jewish law required in restitution.

What did Jesus mean when He called Zacchaeus a "true son of Abraham"?

_____

_____

_____

_____

_____

The place He picks is Jericho, the person He picks is Zacchaeus, and the piece of his life He disturbs is his rejection.

EVERYONE

That Jesus would go to Samaria, a place where no other Jews would go, for just one woman is amazing! That He would go to Peter's house just to heal his mother-in-law is nice. That He would go to Zacchaeus' house, a place no other Rabbi would go because he was such a disreputable man, is incredible!

That God would come to earth for us—*for you*—and that the God of Heaven would wrap Himself in flesh, come here, dwell among us, and then choose a place like the cross to display His love for us is almost too much to comprehend. That Jesus would disturb the one piece that separates us from a relationship with God the Father on the cross, *intentionally for all of us*, is the most upsetting thing that has ever happened in all of human history.

Besides the separating of time periods before and after Jesus' life, what are some other things that demonstrate the profound influence Jesus had on humanity?

_____

_____

_____

_____

_____

IT'S OUR TURN

Now it's our turn. We don't forgive people of their sins; Jesus has already done that. But we can disturb the piece that's blocking them from seeing the love of God in their lives. We are commissioned to go out and do it. It's not hard. It can actually be a lot of fun. And it starts with you intentionally picking the place.

What are some places that you might consider looking for people to disturb their piece?

_____

_____

_____

_____

_____

Sometimes I disturb people's piece the first time I meet them. Other times, it's the ninth time. There may be an opportunity where the Holy Spirit just gives me a sense of what's going on in their lives. He points out some fear, some intimidation, some rejection, some instability, and then He says, "I want you to disturb *that*!"

As upsetters, we all need to answer the question, "How do I disturb the piece?" How do we determine what are the places, people, and pieces that we are going to disturb?

_____

_____

_____

_____

_____

Who leads us to these places, people, and pieces?

_____

_____

_____

_____

_____

Will you go out and disturb the piece? Because if we all do it, we'll be doing what God put us on earth to do, and it's how we're going to upset the world.

Activation

- Ask God, "Whose piece do you want me to disturb this week?"
- Practice listening to the Holy Spirit and obeying His voice.

CHAPTER 9
UPSETTERS GET USED TO UPSETTING PEOPLE

Lord, help me upset people every day and everywhere I go.

Key Scriptures: Matthew 8:28-34

I didn't do anything more than say hello and use my Uber driver's name, but I upset Bilal's world so much that it gave me an opportunity to talk with him. I found out he was from Lebanon and was driving for Uber to make extra money to provide for his family. He also asked a lot about me, so I shared about Embassy City and told him a little about myself and my family. The end result of that inter-action was that Bilal offered to give free rides to church to anybody who needed one.

All because I wrote "Hi Bilal." in a text message.

Why did Halal respond the way he did to my using his name and being kind and respectful with him? How did it "upset" him?

_____

_____

_____

_____

If we'll be this way in our interactions with people, they'll see Jesus in us, and this will upset them. **Remember, if we do good, the Holy Spirit will bring people to Jesus.**

What are some simple, easy ways you can bless people?

_____

_____

_____

_____

SOME PEOPLE DON'T WANT TO BE UPSET

It was in Jesus' nature to be an upsetter wherever He went. If we're Christ followers, we're naturally going to be upsetting people. Even people who don't want to be upset.

This isn't anything new. Jesus also had to get used to upsetting people, even those who didn't want to be upset.

Read Matthew 8:28–34. What was the nature of the two demon-possessed men Jesus encountered in this passage? What were they doing to the people in the town?

_____

_____

_____

_____

What did the demons ask Jesus? What do you think the demons meant by "before the appointed time"?

_____

_____

_____

_____

Why do you think the demons asked to be sent into the herd of pigs?

_____

_____

_____

_____

After the herd of pigs drowned, the entire town came out to meet Jesus, but it wasn't to thank Him for saving these two men. It wasn't to celebrate their healing. It was just the opposite. They begged Him to go away and leave them alone.

Why do you think the people asked Jesus to leave after He healed the demon-possessed men? Do you think they were grateful to Jesus for eliminating this threat from the town? Explain.

_____

_____

_____

_____

Some people don't want you to upset their world. They like it the way it is. They are so used to their lifestyle that even though they just saw the most amazing miracle, they want things to stay the same. Change can be uncomfortable and shocking. If it looks like it's going to be too much work for people if things change or it gets too uncomfortable, they just might ask you to leave.

Why do you think the woman whose groceries I paid for during my trip to California acted the way she did, even though I was just blessing her?

_____

_____

_____

_____

Have you ever been in a situation where you tried to bless someone and they reacted negatively? Explain.

_____

_____

_____

_____

Have you been in a situation where you were randomly blessed by someone else? How did you feel and how did you respond?

_____

_____

_____

_____

SOME PEOPLE DO WANT TO BE UPSET

Consider these two examples of Jesus upsetting people. In one scenario, Jesus walks through a town, He sees two men who have demons, they recognize him, and He casts them out. They run and tell everyone in the village, and the people are like, "Nope, we're not interested in that." So Jesus leaves. In another, He meets a woman who had a lot of relationships and can't figure out why. He talks to her, she drops her water bucket, goes back to the village, and tells her story of hope and healing to everyone, and the whole city comes to find Jesus. *They wanted to be upset.* They knew her and the kind of person she was before she had her life upset, and they knew if Jesus could do that for her, He could it for them too.

How did the waitress react when my best friend, Korey, and I tipped the waitress $40 for our dinner one evening?

_____

_____

_____

_____

_____

The reality is you upset some people, and they receive it. You upset other people, and they don't receive it. It's not our assignment to size up people and figure out who's going to receive it and who's not. It's simply our assignment to upset.

UPSETTERS GET OTHERS TO UPSET PEOPLE

One of my favorite places to shop is a boutique clothing store in Southlake, Texas, just outside of Dallas, called Zar. The store is owned by Roy, a wonderfully nice Pakistani man who is a Muslim.

A couple of years ago I stopped by the store to browse, and I noticed a young man named Chris trying on a suit for a new job he had just started. It looked great on him and would likely have been perfect for his new position. He told John, one of Roy's salesmen, that he would come back to purchase it in a few weeks when he had saved up the money. I offered to buy the suit for Chris. Even though

I had asked Roy and John not to tell him my name, after some badgering they finally gave him my name and phone number. Chris tracked me down, and we eventually had lunch and a nice conversation.

What happened about a year after my lunch with Chris? Do you think the meeting with his parents was just a random occurrence? Explain.

_____

_____

_____

_____

_____

The family went back home, started a small group in their neighborhood, and about 18 months later, Chris's mother, Michelle, started a ministry called Rise and Go to help disenfranchised kids in the community. I also was able to share the gospel with the kids at an area event she sponsored in September 2018. She wanted them to be upset in the same way she had been upset.

Upset people get others to upset people. Even if they don't become Christians immediately from your influence and example.

How did the guys at Zar demonstrate their being upset?

_____

_____

_____

_____

_____

Describe a situation where someone's behavior changed for the better because they were blessed by you or someone you know.

_____

_____

_____

_____

_____

Activation

- Ask yourself, "How do I respond when people try to bless me?"
- Ask the Holy Spirit to send you someone to upset this week.

CHAPTER 10
UPSETTERS UPSET THE WORLD

Holy Spirit, go with me as I follow Your command to upset the world. Amen.

Key Scriptures: 1 Corinthians 3:6–7; Romans 5:8; Matthew 28:16–20

When I followed the serviceman from security to his gate at the St. Louis Airport, two things crossed my mind. One, I wanted to obey what the Lord was telling me to do. And two, I wanted to upset this guy's world. I put the gift card under his headphones on the seat and walked away without engaging in conversation after he replied, "Thank you." I didn't wait around and spend time witnessing to him. I was just planting a seed.

UPSETTERS SOW SEEDS

"Reaping the harvest" is an expression taken from Matthew 9:37–38 when Jesus said to His disciples, "The harvest is great, but the workers are few. So pray to the Lord who is in charge of the harvest; ask him to send more workers into his fields." I've noticed, more so in recent years, that there's a romanticism with the harvest and winning souls, but seedtime and irrigation have almost been forgotten.

Read Matthew 9:27–36. What kinds of upsetting acts had Jesus performed just prior to talking about the harvest in verse 37?

_____

_____

_____

In verse 30, what did Jesus tell the blind men NOT to do after He healed them? Did they obey Him? How does this event demonstrate the principles of upsetting we've discussed in previous chapters?

_____

_____

_____

_____

_____

In verse 34, how did the crowds react to Jesus casting out a demon and restoring the man's speech? What does this say about how they were upset?

_____

_____

_____

_____

_____

How did the Pharisees try to explain how Jesus was able to cast out demons? Does it make any sense? What does their effort to explain His miracles say about how they were upset?

_____

_____

_____

_____

_____

Verse 35 says Jesus went through all the villages teaching and healing every kind of disease and illness. According to verse 36, what was the main reason for Jesus doing these things?

_____

_____

_____

_____

_____

Considering these events, what does what Jesus said in verses 37–38 imply about the type of seeds we can plant and how we can plant them?

_____

_____

_____

_____

_____

My wife, Juliette, has a garden in our backyard. She puts in fresh soil, plants the seeds, waters the plants as they grow, pulls weeds, and makes sure the garden gets plenty of sunlight. She lets nothing go to waste, not even the weeds. She pulls them up, lets them dry until they turn brown, and then puts them in the compost machine. She then takes the compost and puts it back into the dirt, giving the soil nutrients that help the plants grow. She meticulously tends to it daily until it is time to gather the harvest.

What could Juliette do if all she was interested in was the harvest? How is this like that attitude of many Christians today?

_____

_____

_____

_____

_____

According to 1 Corinthians 3:6–7, who gets credit for the increase of the harvest?

_____

_____

_____

_____

_____

What actions are sowing and watering analogous to when talking about evangelism?

_____

_____

_____

_____

_____

Read Matthew 13:3–8. Should we be selective about where we sow the seed of the gospel (who we try to reach for Christ)? Whose job is it to make the seed stick and explain faith to people to whom we have thrown the seeds of the gospel? Explain.

_____

_____

_____

_____

Consider my experience with the girl who does my pedicures. What was her opinion of churches since she had moved to Texas from California?

_____

_____

_____

_____

What do you think would have been her response if I had tried to argue or convince her that she needed to come to church?

_____

_____

_____

_____

If we are going to upset the world, we have to bring the gospel message to _____

_____.

UPSETTERS SHOW PEOPLE HOW
TO CHANGE THEIR CLOTHES

One of the most fascinating parables Jesus ever told is about the great feast in Matthew 22:1–14. He was talking to the religious leaders of His day, the ones who had moved away from the type of relationship God wanted to establish when He brought them out of Egypt so they could worship Him and have a one-on-one relationship with Him. But He's also talking to us.

In verse 2, what does Jesus say the great wedding feast illustrates?

_____

_____

_____

_____

_____

In verses 3–4, how many times did the king have his servants invite the guests?

_____

_____

_____

_____

_____

Verses 5 and 6 describe how the first batch of guests reacted. How are the actions of the invited guests comparable to the ways that people today might reject the gospel?

_____

_____

_____

_____

What does the king do to the guests who seized and killed his messengers in verse 6? To what group of people might we compare those "murderers" today in the context of spreading the gospel?

_____

_____

_____

_____

All of these people, unintended guests, show up to this party. When the king comes down to meet them, he notices one of the guests doesn't have on the right clothes.

Why did the king expect all the guests to be wearing certain clothes once they entered the banquet hall?

_____

_____

_____

_____

You see, the invitation is "come as you are," but the implication is "you can't stay as you are." The invitation is "all are welcome," but the invitation is also "you can't stay the same." So when the king comes down, and everyone has changed their clothes except this one man, it implies that he is filled with obstinance and rebellion. Truthfully, this man's "no reply" *is* a reply.

Who, in this story, does the king represent? What group does the initial group of invited guests represent? After that group rejected the invitation, what group of people are represented by the open invitation (see Romans 5:8)?

_____

_____

_____

_____

What one thing does Jesus expect of someone He calls?

_____

_____

_____

_____

According to Romans 13:12–14, what does Jesus expect will happen to us once we accept His call?

_____

_____

_____

_____

"Come as you are" is the evangelistic message of the gospel, but "you can't stay as you are" is the discipleship message of the gospel. We want everyone to come, but we don't want anybody to stay the same. There is something happening in 2019 Christianity that we want people in church so badly that we won't even tell them to change their clothes. We want people to be in community and in our churches, but we don't want to offend anyone. So we say, "Whatever you have on is fine. I don't care what it is; it's fine." And that's true ... **whatever you have on is fine enough for you to come to Jesus, but it won't be good enough for you to stay here.**

Whose choice is it to obey God or remain a slave to sin? Does God *make* someone change? Can we make someone change? What role do we play in helping someone come to the cross?

_____

_____

_____

_____

YOUR ASSIGNMENT

Read Matthew 28:16–20. Who has the Lord called to go and make disciples; to "Go Upset the World"?

How much authority do we have in going to upset the world? What is the realm of that authority?

_____

_____

_____

_____

An upsetter is someone who's been upset and upsets others. Here's how Paul says it in 2 Timothy 2:2:

> You have heard me teach things that have been confirmed by many reliable witnesses. Now teach these truths to other trustworthy people who will be able to pass them on to others.

How can we plainly know that we are to upset the world? What is the one main thing that each of us must do to upset the world?

_____

_____

_____

_____

I hope this book has equipped you with everything you need to upset the world and that you would be bold and, through the Holy Spirit, go out and upset others with the message, hope, and love of Jesus Christ. Don't let anything or anyone stop what God has called you to do. **Expressing your faith can change the world.**

Consider your role in the process of upsetting the world. To whom can you scatter a handful of seeds? What is your assignment each day; sowing, watering or harvesting?

_____

_____

_____

_____

Activation

- Read Matthew 22:1–14. Ask yourself, "Do I need to change my clothes?"
- Plant and water some gospel seeds as you go about life this week. You never know how God might use you to upset someone's world.

EPILOGUE

Lord, when times get hard,
help me remember Your plans for my life. Amen.

Key Scriptures: Jeremiah 29:11; Ephesians 2:10

As you start out on your journey to upset the world, I want to make sure you go out with the knowledge and understanding of how much God loves you and that He has great plans for your life. When the enemy comes against you—and he will—and tries to overthrow you, you can stand with your feet firmly planted on this Scripture:

> "For I know the plans I have for you," says the Lord. "They are plans for good and not for disaster, to give you a future and a hope" (Jeremiah 29:11).

What does Jeremiah 29:11 mean to you, in your own words?

_____

_____

_____

_____

Read Ephesians 2:10. How does God describe us in one word? For what purpose has He "created us anew"?

_____

_____

_____

_____

This can be difficult for us to do, knowing the good and bad things about ourselves. However, 2 Corinthians 5:17 tell us that we *are* new creations. His plans for each one of us are to be strategically used in the place of our expertise, the place of our passion to reach people for His name.

And that's really the reason we're all here: to upset the world with the message, hope, and love of Jesus Christ. If you get this, you *will* upset the world.